The Tale Of The Cell

Written by Georgene' Glass.

Melanin Origins

Published by Melanin Origins LLC
PO Box 122123; Arlington, TX 76012

First Edition

Library of Congress Control Number: 2021900455

ISBN: 978-1-62676-544-3 hardback
ISBN: 978-1-62676-591-7paperback
ISBN: 978-1-62676-590-0 ebook

This book is dedicated to all the children and families affected by Sickle Cell Disease.

To my daughters Raven and Gia, I hope this book serves as inspiration and motivation to follow your dreams. Always speak up for yourself, and never be ashamed of who you are.

To my mother who instilled my love of reading and writing, I hope you are looking down from heaven and can see that I actually was listening all that time.

To my favorite cousin Jennifer, thank you for always being there for me and the girls, and supporting my ideas even when they seemed far-fetched.

Last but certainly not least, Jamie, thank you for giving me the gift that keeps giving, my miracle child (Gia) that has led to this journey to make sure our baby has a fair chance at life with whatever she does. Thank you for being a silent supporter making it possible for me to always be with Gia whenever she may need me for however long that may be.

To everyone who has supported me on this journey, all the Warriors I've met along the way, the ones we've lost , my DJ, Jewel, and countless others, your courage, your strength inspires people like me to fight with you .

I vow to do my part for as long as there is breath in my body to #MakeSickleCellPopular

Hi, I'm Gia and I have sickle cell anemia (ss), also known as sickle cell disease or SCD depending on who you talk to.

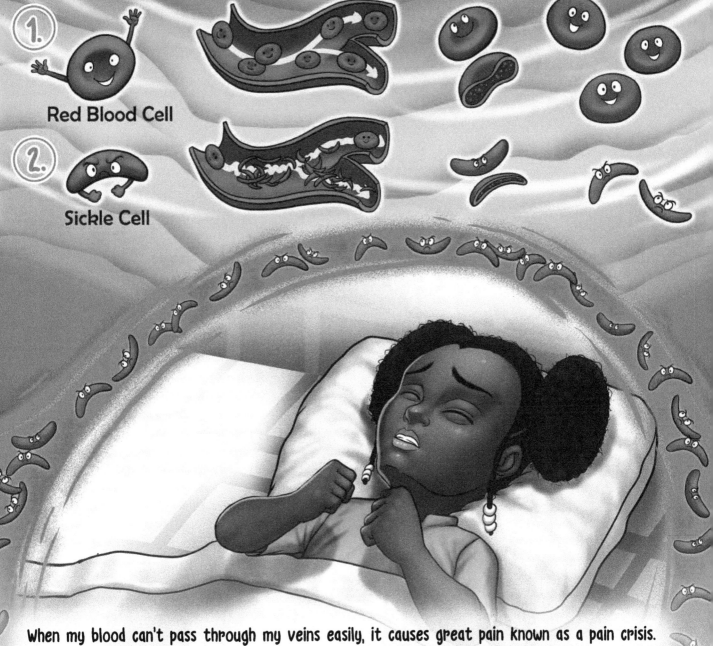

1. Red Blood Cell

2. Sickle Cell

When my blood can't pass through my veins easily, it causes great pain known as a pain crisis. When my body is working properly my blood looks like the first picture. When my blood begins to sickle and cause me to have pain, it looks like the second picture inside my body.

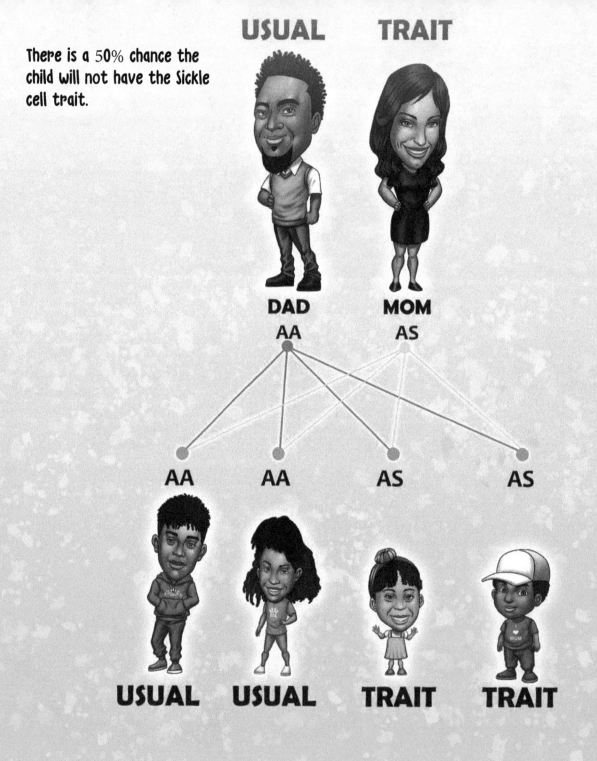

There is a 50% chance the child will not have the Sickle cell trait.

USUAL   TRAIT

DAD   MOM
AA   AS

AA   AA   AS   AS

USUAL   USUAL   TRAIT   TRAIT

How do you get sickle cell you ask? Sickle Cell is an inherited genetic disease.

Unaffected "Carrier" Father

Unaffected "Carrier" Mother

A S   A S

A A   A S   A S   S S

Unaffected
1 in 4 chance

Unaffected "Carrier"
1 in 4 chance

Affected
1 in 4 chance

My older sister Raven and I have different fathers and, though we share the same awesome mom who has the Sickle Cell Trait (SCT), Raven neither has the trait or the disease.

This is my cousin Reniya who also has Sickle Cell Disease, just a different type (SC). She got one "S" gene from her mother my big cousin, and a "C" gene from her father. I got an S from mom and an S from dad, which is why my type is "SS". My mother is her mom's aunt, isn't that cool? We are different, yet the same.

Here is a little secret about me – I love food! Yes, sweets taste the best, but fruits and veggies keep a warrior like me healthy. I also love drinking lots of water. It is very important to stay hydrated when you have SCD.

Splish! Splash! I love to swim. As much as I enjoy the water , I can't stay too long or get in when it's too cold. Not unless I want to have a pain crisis, and those are no fun.

Achew! Catching colds for me is easy to do, but hard to get rid of. If it lingers too long I may end up in the hospital. They have some fun toys there, but nothing like the toys I have at home!

After a few days in the hospital, I am as good as new and back to all my fun activities like driving my fancy ride.

Types of Sickle Cell

Hemoglobin SS Diseases

Hemoglobin SS disease is the most common type of Sickle Cell disease.It occurs when you inherit copies of the hemoglobin S gene from bothparents. This forms hemoglobin know as Hb SS. As the most severe form of SCD, individuals with this form also experience the worst symptoms at a higher rate.

Hemogloblin SC Diseases

Hemoglobin SC disease is the second most common type of Sickle Cell disease.It occurs when you inherit the Hb C gene from one parent and the Hb S geneFrom the other. Individuals with Hb SC have similar symptoms to individualswith Hb SS. However, the anemia is less severe.

Hemogloblin SB+ (Beta) Diseases

Hemoglobin SB+ (beta) thalassemia affects beta globin gene production.The size of the red blood cell is reduced because less beta protein is made.If inherrited with the Hb S gene, you will have hemoglobin S beta Thalassemia. Symptoms are not severe.

Hemogloblin SB 0 (Beta-Zero) Diseases

Hemoglobin SB 0 (Beta-Zero) thalassemia is the fourth type of Sickle Cell disease. It also involves the beta globin gene. It has similar symptoms to Hb SS anemia However, sometimes the symptoms of beta zero thalassemia are more severe.
It is associated with a poorer prognosis.

Hemoglobin SD, hemoglobin SE, And Hemoglobin SO

These types of Sickle Cell dieases are more rare and usually don't have Severe symptoms.

Sickle Cell Trait

People who only inherit a mutated gene (hemoglobin S) from one parentare said to have Sickle Cell trait. They may have no symtoms or reduced symptoms.

Complications of Sickle Cell

Frequent colds and infections

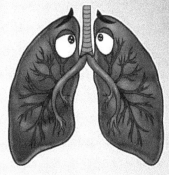

Acute Chest Syndrome (ACS)/Pneumonia

Pain Crises

Fatigue

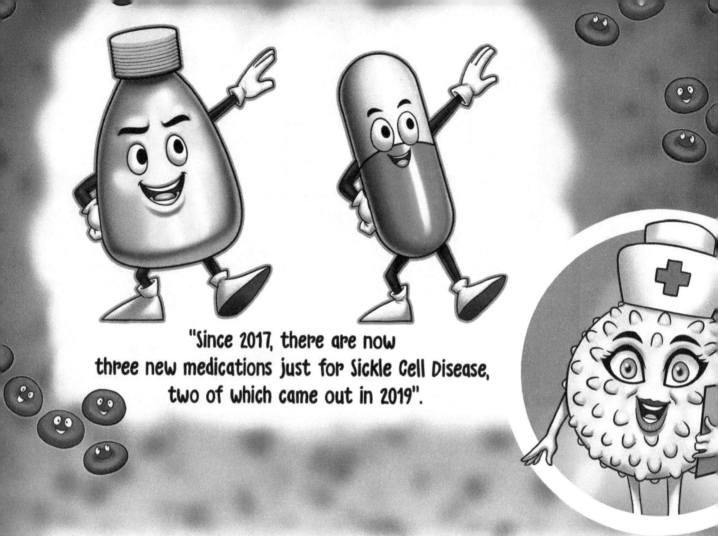

"Since 2017, there are now three new medications just for Sickle Cell Disease, two of which came out in 2019".

Aside from eating healthy foods, I also take medicines prescribed by a doctor and add in a few vitamins. Penicillin (pehznuhzsizluhn) and Amoxicillin (uhzmaakzsuhzsizluhn) antibiotics are medications prescribed by a physician to help manage infections common to Sickle Cell Disease. However, Hydroxyurea pronounced (Hi-drox-urEa) is currently the only FDA approved medication to manage the symptoms of Sickle Cell. In 2014 it was recommended that this medication be given to infants starting at nine months as a preventative method to reduce the complications of sickle cell.

*As always, please consult your treating Physician / Hematologist before taking any natural or prescribed medications.

There currently is no universal cure for Sickle Cell Disease. Bone marrow transplant has cured many with Sickle Cell Disease and there are many therapies just for us on the horizon.

Right now , I am too young for much of what's out there that may cure Sickle Cell. But soon I'll be old enough for my chance at a cure!

Right now, the best way to help kids like me is by donating blood. Most African Americans have O type blood. There is always a shortage on this type . I am actually type A but most of my fellow warriors really need O blood , it helps us stay healthy and get healthy when we are sick.

Who has Sickle Cell Disease? Anyone can inherit Sickle Cell Disease; we come in many colors, shapes and sizes. Can you tell which one of us has SCD? Here are a few facts about us:

• Any race can be affected by Sickle Cell Disease or carry the trait.
• SCD affects approximately 100,000 Americans.
• SCD occurs among about 1 out of every 365 Black or African-American births.
• SCD occurs among about 1 out of every 16,300 Hispanic-American births.
• About 1 in 13 Black or African-American babies is born with sickle cell trait (SCT).

Did you guess which of us has SCD yet? We all do!

We run, we laugh , we play, this is true. The way we look, the things we do, are just the same as you!

Important dates to remember
June 19th – World Sickle Cell Day
September – Sickle Cell Awareness Month

Foundations Dedicated to Sickle Cell Awareness
Dreamsickle Kids Foundation , Nevada-www.dreamsicklekids.org
SCDAA, National-www.sicklecelldisease.org
Carols Promise Sickle Cell Organization,Texas- www.carolspromise.org

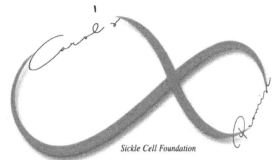

Sickle Cell Foundation

About the Author

Georgene Glass is a mother of two from Southern California. After her youngest daughter was born with Sickle Cell Disease, she relocated her family to Nevada. It was there she decided to create what would be the first Sickle Cell organization in the state. For the past five years she has dedicated her life to advocating for those in Nevada and across the US impacted by Sickle Cell Disease. One day in 2018 she decided to write a children's book about Sickle Cell and a few years later it has now evolved into The Tale of The Cell. Through her advocacy for Sickle Cell Disease, it is her hope that one day children and adults alike will see a cure for this painful illness.

CPSIA information can be obtained
at www.ICGtesting.com
Printed in the USA
BVHW061321220421
605633BV00007B/1394

9 781626 765443